APR 2008

ELLA JOHNSON MEMORIAL
PUBLIC LIBRARY DISTRICT
109 S. STATE ST.
HAMPSHIRE, IL 60140
(847) 683-4490

DEMCO

First Ladies

Betty
Ford

Joanne Mattern

ABDO
Publishing Company

visit us at
www.abdopublishing.com

Published by ABDO Publishing Company, 8000 West 78th Street, Edina, Minnesota 55439.
Copyright © 2008 by Abdo Consulting Group, Inc. International copyrights reserved in all
countries. No part of this book may be reproduced in any form without written permission from
the publisher. The Checkerboard Library™ is a trademark and logo of ABDO Publishing
Company.

Printed in the United States.

Cover Photo: Courtesy Gerald Ford Presidential Library
Interior Photos: Corbis pp. 5, 17, 18, 19, 22, 23; Courtesy Gerald Ford Presidential Library pp. 7,
    8, 9, 10, 11, 12, 13, 15, 21, 24; Getty Images pp. 25, 27, 31

Series Coordinator: BreAnn Rumsch
Editors: Rochelle Baltzer, BreAnn Rumsch
Art Direction & Cover Design: Neil Klinepier

Library of Congress Cataloging-in-Publication Data

Mattern, Joanne, 1963-
  Betty Ford / Joanne Mattern.
    p. cm. -- (First ladies)
  Includes index.
  ISBN-13: 978-1-59928-794-2
  1. Ford, Betty, 1918---Juvenile literature. 2. Presidents' spouses--United States--Biography--
Juvenile literature. I. Title.
  E867.M38 2007
  973.925092--dc22
  [B]
                                                              2007009725

Contents

Betty Ford

Betty Ford never expected to become a First Lady. Her husband, Gerald R. Ford, was the thirty-eighth president of the United States. But, he was not elected president. Instead, Vice President Ford became president when President Richard Nixon resigned. He was appointed to finish Nixon's term from 1974 to 1977.

President Ford was in office for a shorter time than most presidents. But, Mrs. Ford made the most of her time as First Lady. And, she became a respected leader of the American people.

Mrs. Ford faced many personal challenges while she was First Lady. But, she did not mind telling the public about her problems. She was not afraid to speak out about topics that a First Lady had never before talked about. Mrs. Ford's honesty helped many people face their own problems, too. This First Lady became a role model in a very special way.

Betty Ford became First Lady through unusual events! At first, she felt unprepared for the job. But eventually, she left her mark on history as one of America's most popular First Ladies.

A Close Family

Elizabeth Anne Bloomer was born in Chicago, Illinois, on April 8, 1918. She was called Betty from the time she was born. Her father, William, worked as a salesman. Her mother, Hortense, stayed home and cared for Betty and her older brothers, Bill Jr. and Bob.

The family moved to Denver, Colorado, shortly after Betty was born. But they didn't live there long. When Betty was two years old, the Bloomers settled in Grand Rapids, Michigan.

Betty's family was very close and did many activities together. Her parents had a lake house where the family spent every summer. There, they enjoyed boating, swimming, and having picnics. Betty and her brothers also liked to explore the nearby woods and play at the beach.

William and Hortense were good parents. They expected their children to be polite and hardworking. They also encouraged them to pursue their interests. So, Betty always felt she could be anything she wanted.

Betty at age three

A Beautiful Dancer

Fourteen-year-old Betty had a big heart. She gave her family the money she earned at her job.

Betty once said she was, "a terrible tomboy." That is because she loved sports. Betty wanted to play football and hockey just like her brothers. So, she often followed them around.

When Betty was eight years old, she started attending dance classes. Betty discovered that she really enjoyed dancing. Soon, she was studying many different kinds of dance. She took tap, ballet, and Spanish dancing lessons. Betty worked hard at her lessons. If she heard about a new kind of dance, she wanted to learn it.

Betty grew into a beautiful teenager. When she was 14 years old, she got a job as a department store model. She would walk through the store modeling clothes that were sold there. Betty also gave dance lessons to children. She charged her students fifty cents for each lesson.

In 1936, Betty graduated from Grand Rapids Central High School. She dreamed of becoming a professional dancer. So, Betty left home for the first time. She spent two summers studying dance at Bennington College in Bennington, Vermont. There, Betty took lessons from Martha Graham. Graham was a famous dancer at the time.

Betty was full of energy and continued to love sports and other games as she grew older.

Away from Home

When Betty was 20 years old, she moved to New York City, New York, to study at Graham's studio. There, Betty worked hard at what she loved. She did not make the principal **troupe**. However, she was selected for a secondary group. To earn money, Betty worked as a model. She loved living in New York City. It was a busy, exciting place.

Eventually, Betty's mother asked her to come home to Michigan. Hortense missed Betty very much. Betty was sad to leave New York. But, she returned to Grand Rapids to start a new life.

Back at home, Betty got a new job at the department store.

22-year-old Betty

Now, she organized fashion shows, trained models, and designed the store windows. Betty enjoyed this job very much. But she did not forget about dancing. Soon, Betty started her own dance company. There, she taught movement to disabled children.

During this time, Betty fell in love with a man named Bill Warren. In 1942, Betty and Bill got married. The couple moved many times during their marriage because Bill often changed jobs. After only a few years, Betty felt that she no longer loved Bill. So in 1947, the couple divorced.

Betty's favorite style of dance was modern dance. This style lets dancers move freely and express themselves in more ways than ballet does.

Late for the Wedding

Betty and Gerald share a moment at their rehearsal dinner.

Betty stayed busy working at the department store in Grand Rapids. She did not want to marry again. Then, a friend introduced her to a man named Gerald Ford. Gerald wanted to date Betty, but she was not interested.

Eventually, Betty agreed to a date. It turned out that she liked Gerald very much. He was five years older than Betty. Gerald had been a star football player at the University of Michigan. Now, he was a lawyer who was interested in politics. He told Betty he planned to run for Congress.

In February 1948, Gerald asked Betty to marry him. Betty said yes right away. The wedding was planned for October 15. There was just one problem. Gerald was so busy campaigning for Congress

that Betty did not see him very much. Gerald even left their wedding rehearsal dinner early to give a speech!

On the day of the wedding, Betty waited for Gerald at the church. Everyone was there except Gerald! He was out campaigning again. Finally, Gerald ran into the church. Betty noticed his shoes were dirty from being on the road, but she did not care. The couple got married just as they had planned.

The newlyweds enjoyed a short honeymoon, since Gerald was still campaigning for Congress.

A Busy Life

A few weeks after the wedding, Mr. Ford was elected to Congress. So, he and his wife moved to Georgetown, Delaware, to be closer to Washington, D.C. Suddenly, Mrs. Ford was a political wife.

Mrs. Ford had a lot to learn about politics. She was expected to host parties and attend social events. She did volunteer work for hospitals and charities. Mrs. Ford also met many government leaders and other important people. And, she helped her husband at his office.

The Fords were also eager to start a family. In 1950, the couple welcomed their first child. They named him Michael. Their second son, John, was born in 1952. Three years later, the family moved to Alexandria, Virginia. There, the Fords had two more children. Steven was born in 1956, and Susan was born in 1957.

Mrs. Ford began spending less time at her husband's office and more time at home. She was busy caring for their children. Family activities included school events and Scouting. The Ford home was also full of pets. The family owned gerbils, turtles, rabbits, and birds. Between the children and the animals, the house was a noisy, exciting place!

Mrs. Ford worked hard to be a good wife and mother. She enjoyed helping her husband with his work. She also played with the children and cared for their home.

Trying Times

Mrs. Ford was glad her husband loved being in Congress. He was reelected several times and became an important congressional leader. Unfortunately, Mr. Ford was away from home a lot because of his job.

One year, Mrs. Ford counted 258 nights that her husband did not come home for dinner! Sometimes an entire week passed before the children saw their father. Mr. Ford tried to call home every night. Still, it was hard for Mrs. Ford and the children to be without him.

In 1964, Mrs. Ford accidentally hurt a nerve in her neck and shoulder. The pain was so bad that she had to go to the hospital. A doctor **prescribed** her a medicine called a painkiller. She took the painkillers every day to feel better.

Mrs. Ford also became sad and lonely when her husband was away. So, she went to a **psychiatrist** to talk about her feelings. Meeting with the psychiatrist helped her.

The doctor advised Mrs. Ford to talk with her husband about how she felt. Mr. Ford then decided it would be better if he did not run for reelection in 1974. However, their lives would soon change in a way they never expected.

Mental health issues were rarely discussed during the 1970s. However, Mrs. Ford encouraged Americans to take care of their minds and their bodies.

An Accidental President

In 1973, Vice President Spiro Agnew was under investigation for taking bribes from people who wanted government jobs. Agnew had broken the law, so he agreed to resign. On December 6, 1973, President Richard Nixon announced that he wanted Mr. Ford to be the new vice president.

With President Nixon's support, Mr. Ford took the oath of office to become the nation's vice president.

Around the same time, President Nixon was also in trouble. He was involved in the **Watergate scandal**. There was evidence that he had covered up a break-in at the Watergate complex in Washington, D.C. Now, Nixon faced **impeachment**. But he did not want to be impeached, so he resigned on August 9, 1974.

When Nixon resigned, Vice President Ford became the nation's new president. Instead of living a quiet life, Mrs. Ford was now the

First Lady of the United States. She was scared about being First Lady. She knew she had a big job. But, Mrs. Ford was determined to do her best. She wanted to be a First Lady who made a difference.

Mrs. Ford was shocked when Vice President Ford became president. Because it happened so suddenly, she joked that he was "an accidental president."

The Chain of Command

The U.S. Constitution includes special instructions that ensure the country will never be without a clear leader. These rules are called the Order of Succession. They explain what to do in case the elected president is no longer able to perform his or her duty. This could be due to an illness, a death, or a resignation.

The Presidential Succession Act of 1947, signed by President Harry S. Truman, set the current order. It states the vice president is second in line for the presidency, followed by the Speaker of the House, the president pro tempore of the Senate, the secretary of state, and the secretary of the treasury. Thirteen other members of the president's cabinet are also included in the list. They are ordered according to the date their office was first established.

In 1967, the Twenty-Fifth Amendment was changed to include a rule for if the vice presidency became vacant. The amendment states that the president is to nominate a new vice president. If Congress agrees with the nomination, that person takes office. In 1973, Gerald Ford was the first vice president to take office under this rule. When President Nixon resigned the next year, Vice President Ford became president according to the Order of Succession.

Straight Talk

Mrs. Ford had always said what was on her mind. This did not change when she became First Lady. She believed that it was important to tell the truth, no matter what. The First Lady also knew that the country was hurting because former president Nixon had lied. The people of the United States needed someone to be honest with them.

Mrs. Ford soon faced a test of her honesty. Only one month after she became First Lady, she learned she had **breast cancer**. In 1974, this disease and its treatments were not publicly discussed. The First Lady decided to change that. She told the American people about her illness. She also told them she would have surgery to remove the cancer.

Women welcomed the First Lady's honesty. Her direct attitude saved many lives. Millions of women took a test to see if they had cancer, too. Mrs. Ford received a lot of support from the American people. That support helped the First Lady get through her own operation and illness.

President Ford supported his wife through her illness. She was happy to have him beside her for her operation at the National Naval Medical Center in Bethesda, Maryland.

Equal Rights

The First Lady had many strong opinions. She believed that men and women should have equal opportunities. Many other people felt the same way. During the 1970s, many women wanted an **equal rights amendment (ERA)** added to the U.S. **Constitution**. Congress passed the amendment in 1972.

Thirty-eight states needed to approve the amendment by 1982 for it to become law. Many people thought the ERA was a bad idea. Some people worried that women would be forced to fight in the military or work outside of the home.

But, the First Lady thought the ERA was a wonderful idea. She told

During her White House years, Mrs. Ford supported many causes. These included the American Heart Association, Goodwill Industries International, and the Washington Hospital for Sick Children.

The ERA was important to many women around the country. Mrs. Ford was one of the movement's most vocal supporters.

reporters she hoped the amendment would pass. She even telephoned state government officials and asked them to pass the law. Some people told the First Lady to mind her own business.

But, Mrs. Ford did not let those people stop her. She continued to work for what she believed in. "I don't believe that being First Lady should prevent me from expressing my ideas," she said. The **ERA** never became a law. Still, Mrs. Ford was proud that she had fought for what she thought was right.

The Betty Ford Center

In 1976, Mr. Ford ran for president of the United States. But, he lost the election to Jimmy Carter. So in 1977, the Fords moved to a new home in Palm Springs, California. However, Mrs. Ford had trouble adjusting to their new life. She missed being First Lady.

Mrs. Ford's family was happy and relieved when she finished the program at the Long Beach Naval Hospital in California.

For many years, Mrs. Ford had been taking painkillers because of her neck injury. Now, she could not stop taking the pills. She also drank too much alcohol. Mr. Ford and their children worried about her. Finally in 1978, they told Mrs. Ford she had to get help for these problems. She agreed to go to a hospital.

Mrs. Ford spent four weeks at a drug and alcohol treatment center. She learned how to deal with her addiction. When she left the hospital, Mrs. Ford decided she wanted to help other people in need get better, too. Once again, Mrs. Ford talked openly about her problems and how she had gotten help.

Mrs. Ford also raised money for a new drug and alcohol treatment center. In 1982, she and her husband opened the Betty Ford Center in Rancho Mirage, California. Today, it is one of the most respected treatment centers in the world.

Mrs. Ford's determination helped her recover from her problems so she could lead a happier life.

Giving Back

The Betty Ford Center first opened its doors in October 1982. The center originally had room for 20 patients in McCallum Hall. One month later, West Hall opened. North Hall opened soon after that. West Hall serves as an all-women's building. In fact, the entire center reserves half of its openings for women.

Today, the Betty Ford Center is considered to have one of the best recovery programs in the United States. It is run by a professional staff, including doctors, counselors, and therapists. Once in a while, Mrs. Ford visits the center to speak to a patient one-on-one. She has said, "I am not qualified to be a professional counselor ... but I can answer a cry for help."

Mrs. Ford's dedication to the center has played a role in its continued success. Not only did she raise most of the money needed to open the Betty Ford Center, but she serves as a board member. She takes the job seriously, speaking with professionals and patients on a regular basis. It is easy to see how important helping others is to Mrs. Ford.

Public Servant

Mrs. Ford continued to stay busy after the Betty Ford Center opened. In 1987, she wrote a book about her recovery titled *A Glad Awakening*. And in the years since, Mrs. Ford has stayed active in public service. She still works for the Betty Ford Center. She also works with groups that help handicapped children. And, she helps organizations promote **breast cancer** awareness, women's issues, and the arts.

Mrs. Ford has received many honors for her work. In October 1999, Mr. and Mrs. Ford were both awarded the Congressional Gold Medal. This award recognized their years of public service.

When Mr. Ford died on December 26, 2006, he was remembered as a great man. At 93, he was the oldest-living president in American history. Mrs. Ford was also honored for changing the role of First Lady. She once called herself, "an ordinary woman who was called onstage at an extraordinary time."

Betty Ford became America's First Lady at a time when the nation was in trouble. But, her commitment to being truthful helped the nation recover from its problems. She also helped millions of people improve their lives by speaking out about her personal troubles. Mrs. Ford used her position as First Lady to connect with others and make life better for people all over America.

Mrs. Ford still spends time talking with people who are living a better life because of the Betty Ford Center.

Timeline

1918	Elizabeth Anne "Betty" Bloomer was born on April 8.
1936	Betty graduated from Grand Rapids Central High School; she began studying dance with Martha Graham at Bennington College.
1942	Betty married Bill Warren.
1947	Betty and Bill divorced.
1948	Betty married Gerald Ford on October 15; Gerald was elected to Congress.
1950	The Fords' first child, Michael, was born.
1952	The Fords' son John was born.
1956	The Fords' son Steven was born.
1957	The Fords' daughter, Susan, was born.
1964	Mrs. Ford suffered a severe neck injury.
1973	Mr. Ford replaced Spiro Agnew as vice president on December 6.
1974	Mrs. Ford was diagnosed with breast cancer.
1974–1977	Mrs. Ford acted as First Lady, while Mr. Ford served as president.
1978	Mrs. Ford spent four weeks at a drug and alcohol treatment center.
1982	The Fords opened the Betty Ford Center.
1987	Mrs. Ford wrote *A Glad Awakening*.
1999	The Fords were awarded the Congressional Gold Medal.
2006	Mr. Ford died on December 26.

Did You Know?

As a young girl, Betty wasn't afraid to stand up to the neighborhood bully.

During her dancing years, Betty was privileged to perform at Carnegie Hall, a famous theater in New York City.

The department store Betty worked for in Michigan was called Herpolsheimer's.

On the first night of their honeymoon, Mr. and Mrs. Ford went to the University of Michigan-Northwestern University football game.

During Gerald Ford's presidential election campaign, some bumper stickers read, "Vote for Betty's husband!"

Mrs. Ford's husband was the only man to serve as president without being elected to either the presidential or vice presidential office.

Mrs. Ford loved to travel. She especially enjoyed her time in Spain, Italy, Russia, Poland, and China.

During her travels around the world, Mrs. Ford began collecting miniature spoons. She also started a doll collection for her daughter, Susan.

Mrs. Ford has written two books. They are *A Glad Awakening* and *The Times of My Life*.

Glossary

breast cancer - a disease characterized by an abnormal growth of cells in a person's breast that destroys healthy tissues and organs.

Constitution - the laws that govern the United States.

equal rights amendment (ERA) - a proposed change to the U.S. Constitution that would guarantee equal rights to males and females.

impeach - to charge a public official with misconduct in office.

prescribe - to order as medicine or treatment.

psychiatrist - a doctor who specializes in identifying and treating mental, emotional, and behavioral disorders.

scandal - an action that shocks people and disgraces those connected with it.

troupe - a group of dancers or actors that travels.

Watergate - a 1972 political crime involving President Richard Nixon. Nixon's aides broke into the Watergate complex to steal campaign information about his opponent. The burglars were caught and sent to jail. Nixon resigned in 1974.

Web Sites

To learn more about Betty Ford, visit ABDO Publishing Company on the World Wide Web at **www.abdopublishing.com**. Web sites about Betty Ford are featured on our Book Links page. These links are routinely monitored and updated to provide the most current information available.

Index